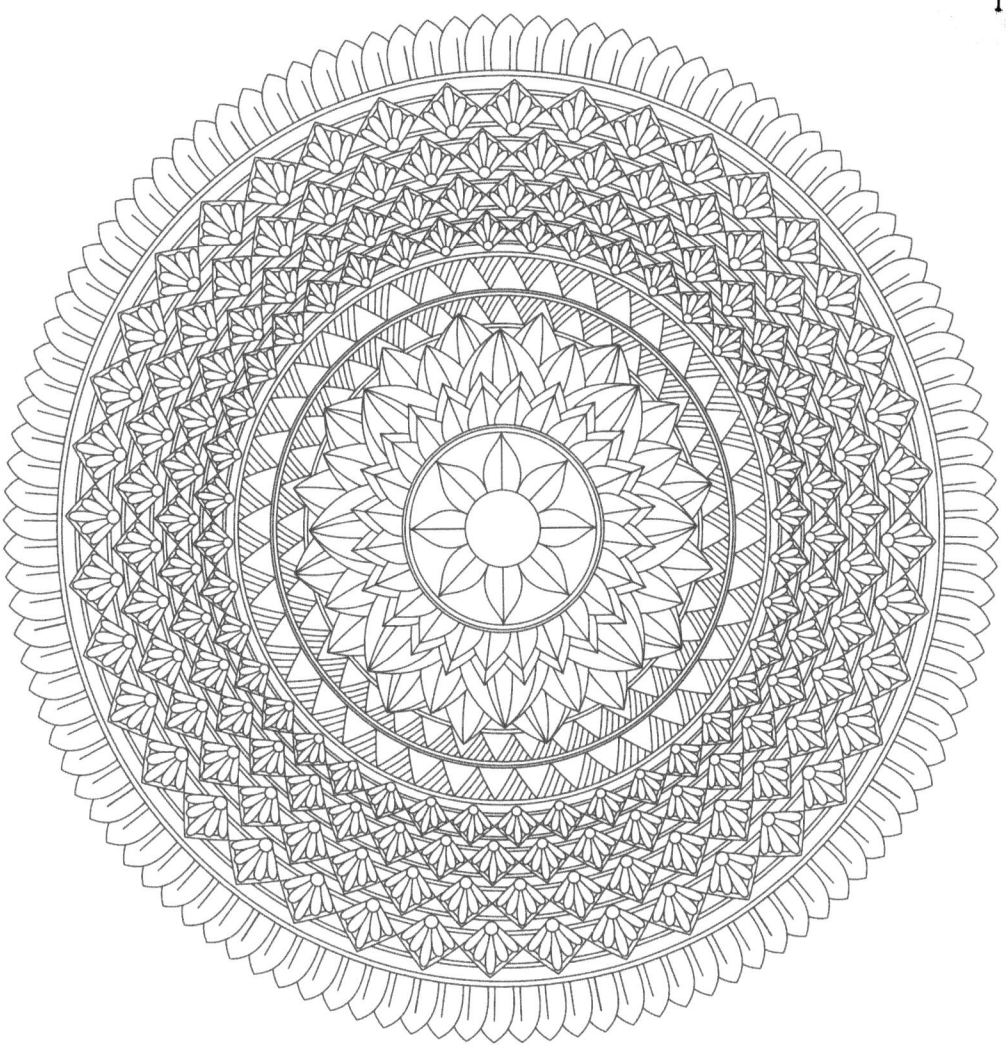

# Relax With Mandalas
## A Coloring Book  Volume 1

Copyright © 2021 by Kimberly C. Hart
All rights reserved

ISBN: 9798733155432

Independently published

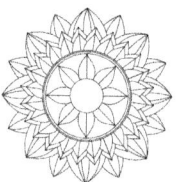

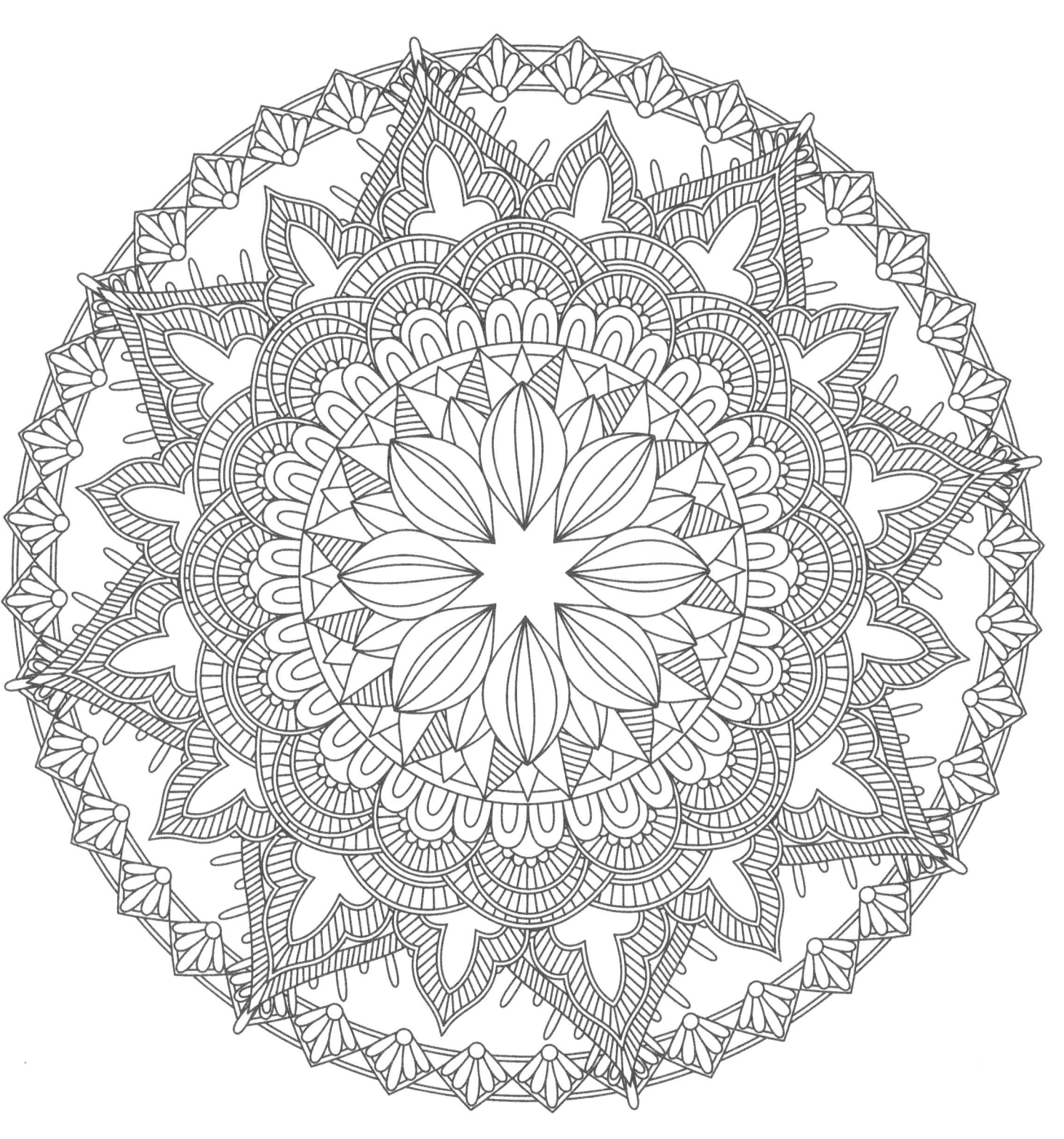

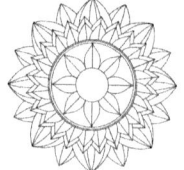

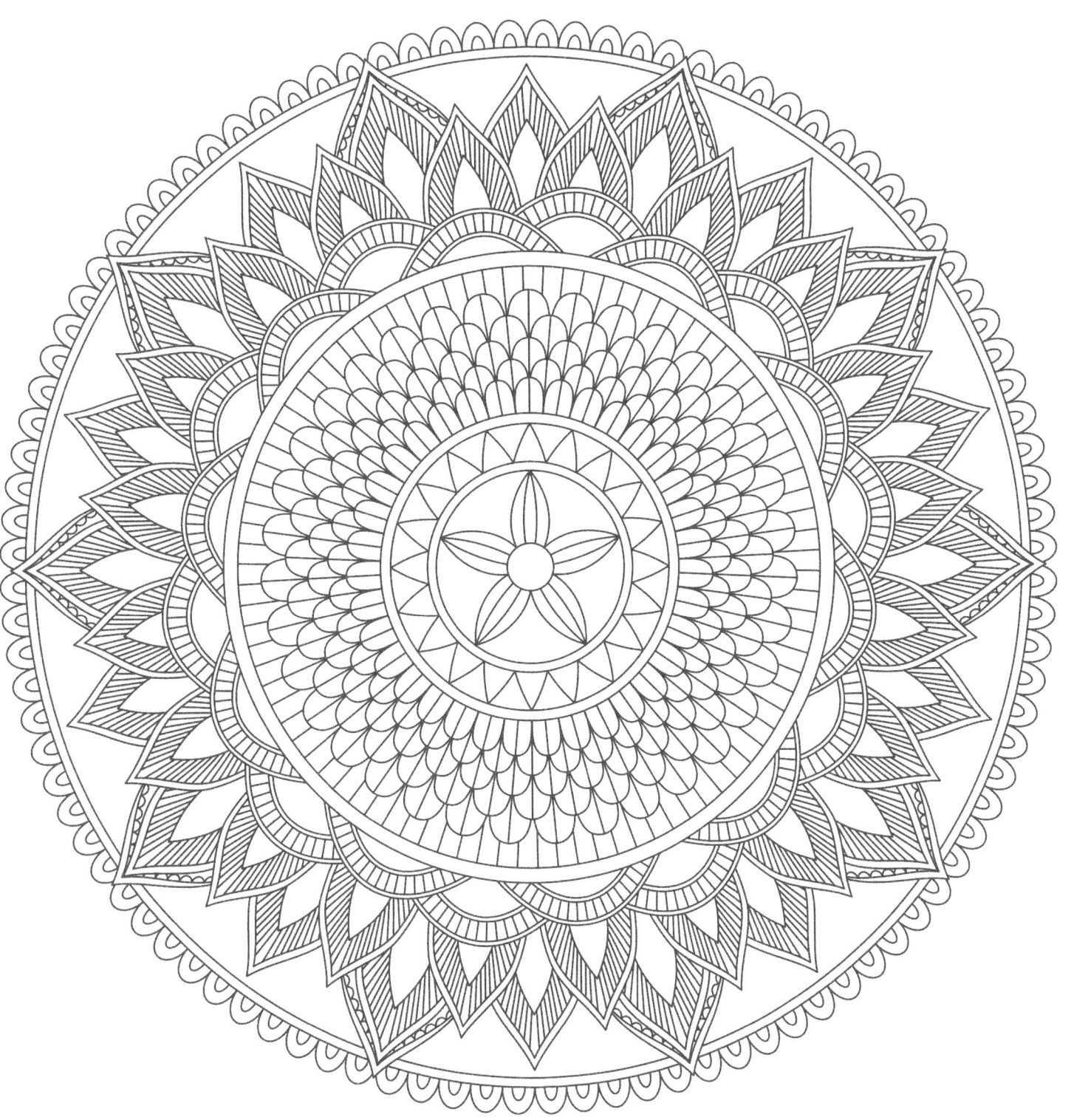

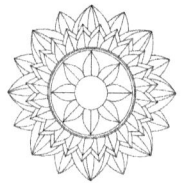

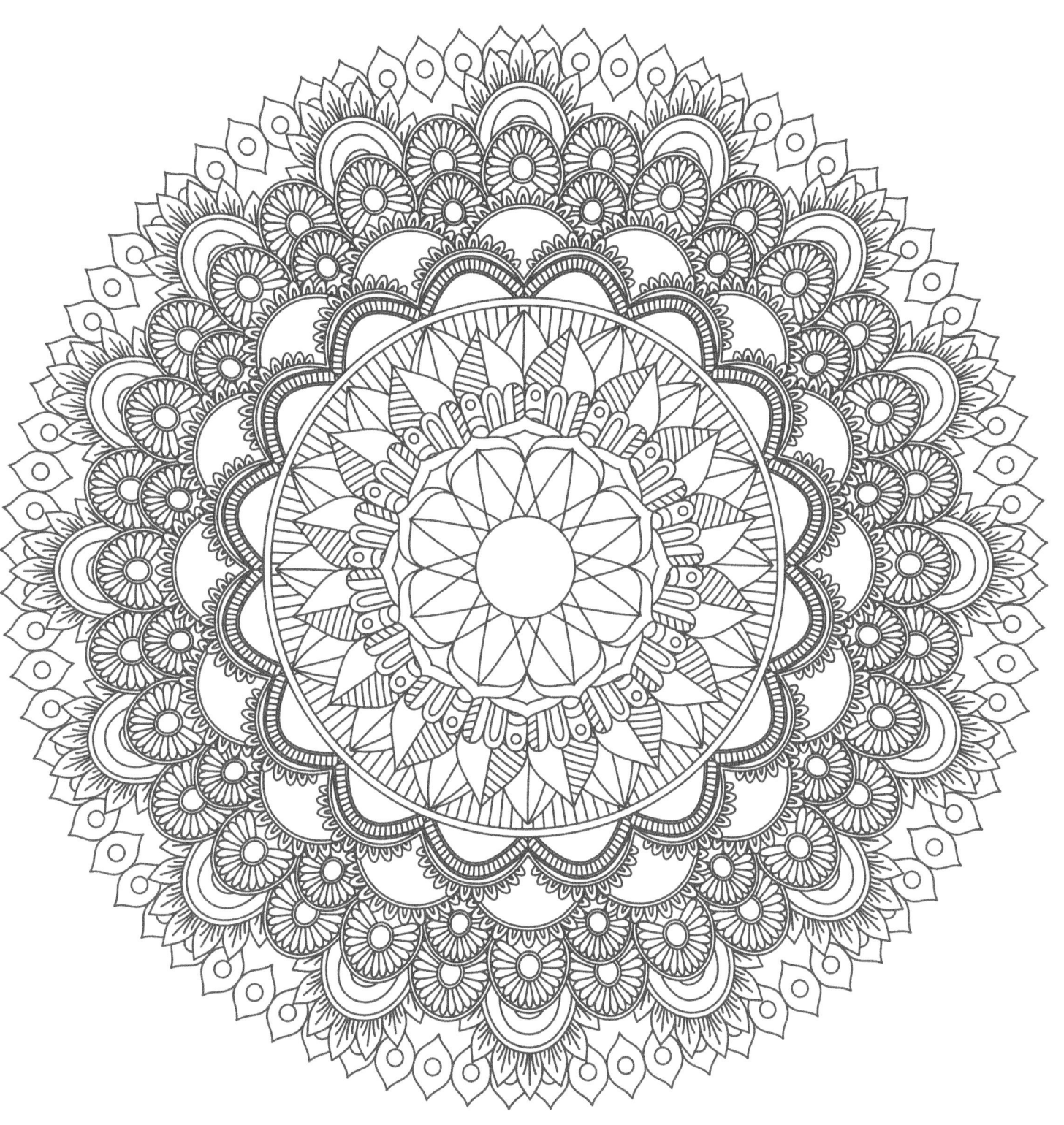

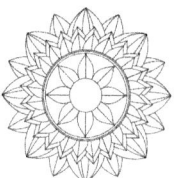

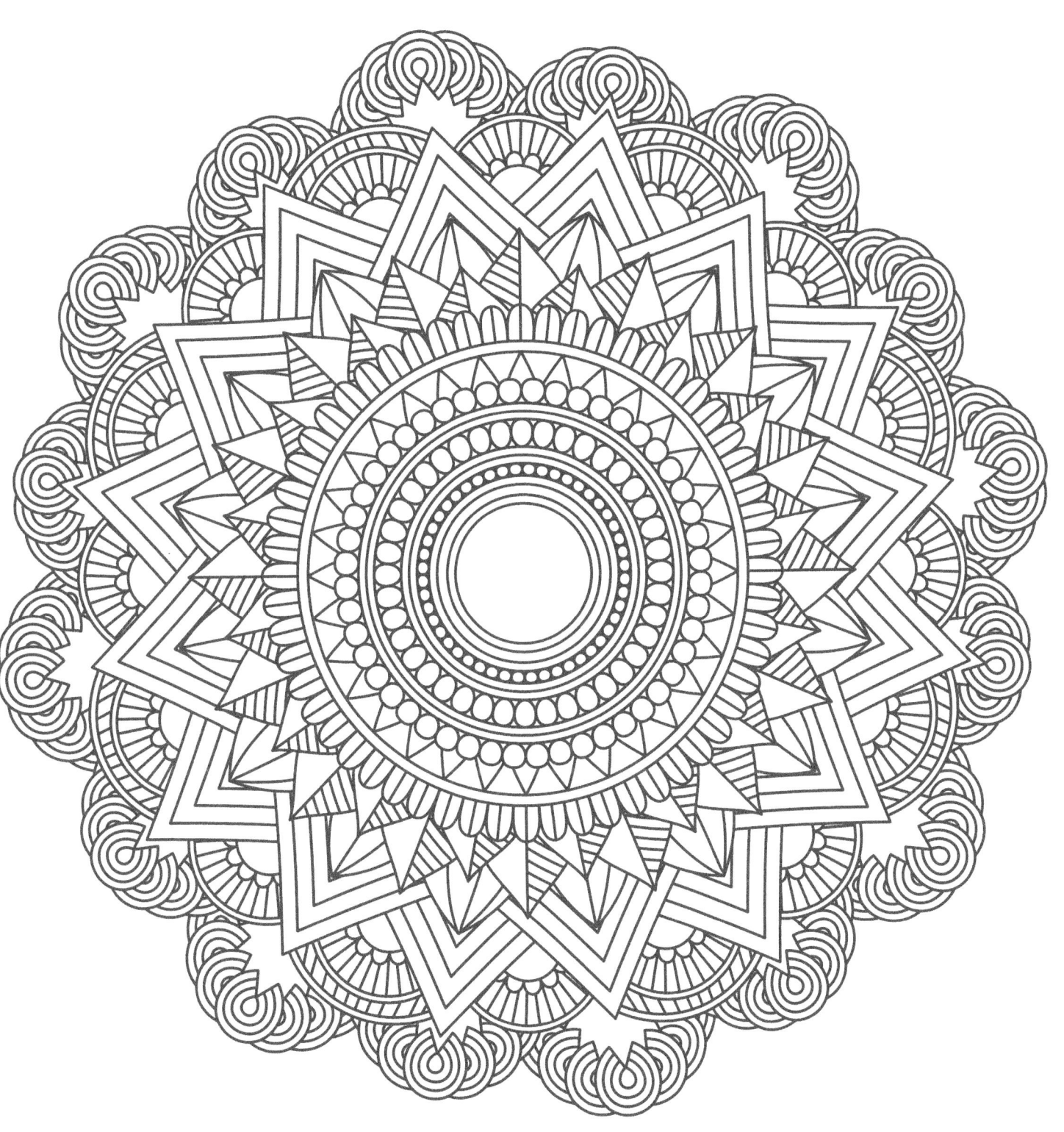

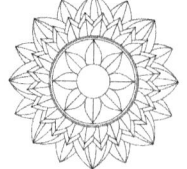

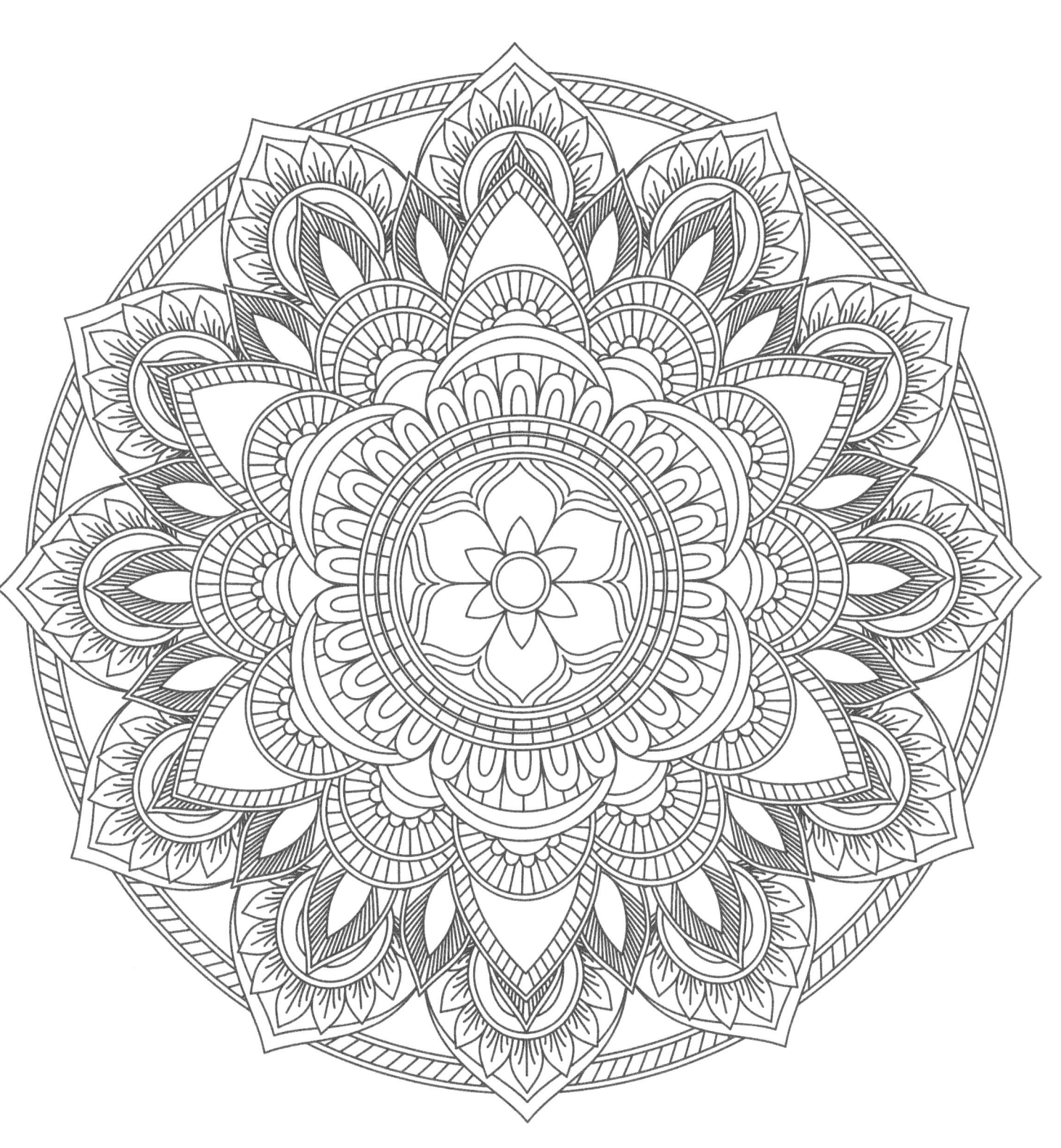

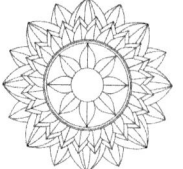

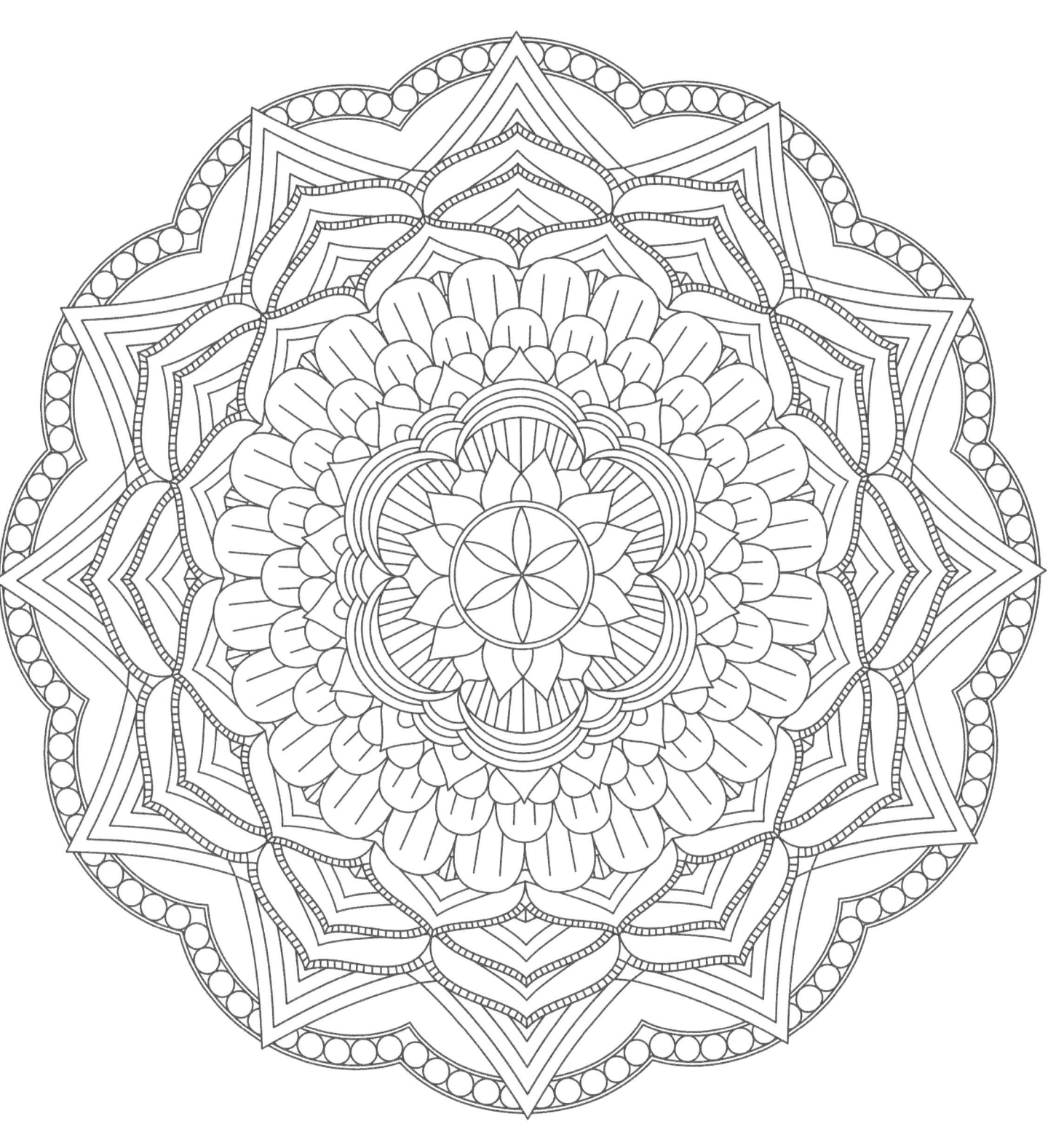

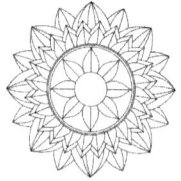

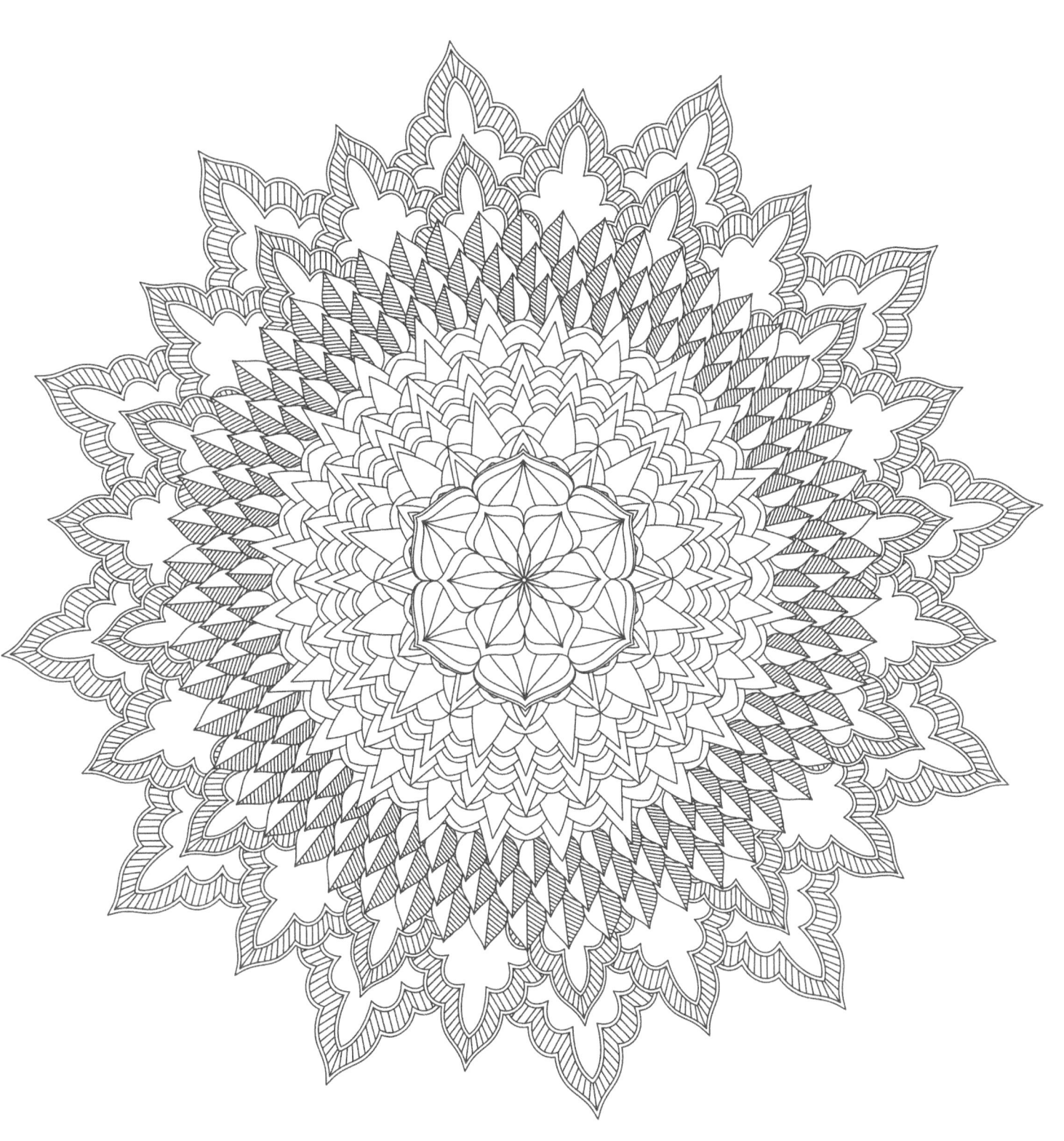

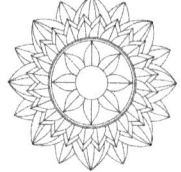

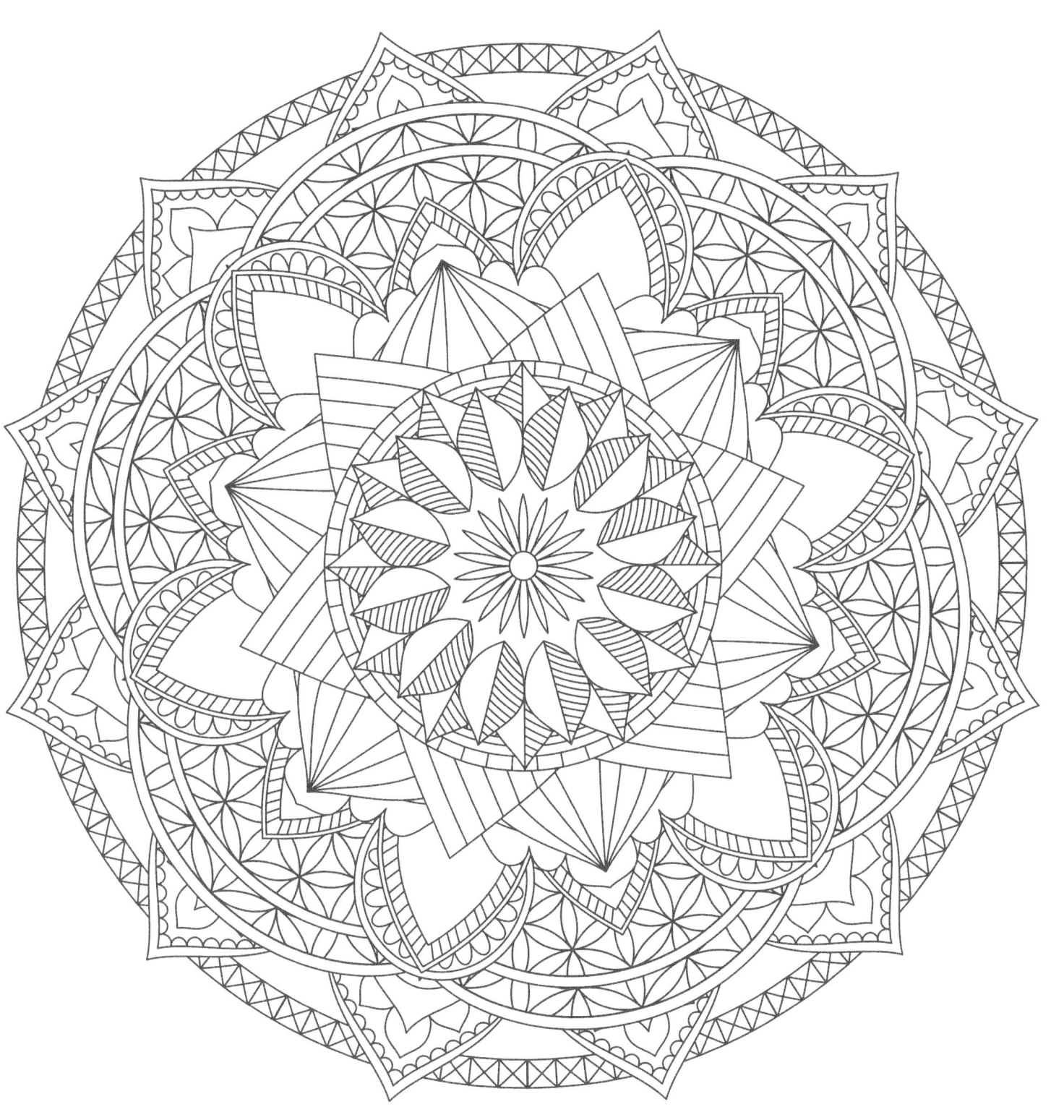

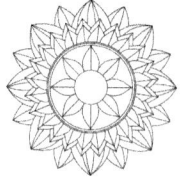

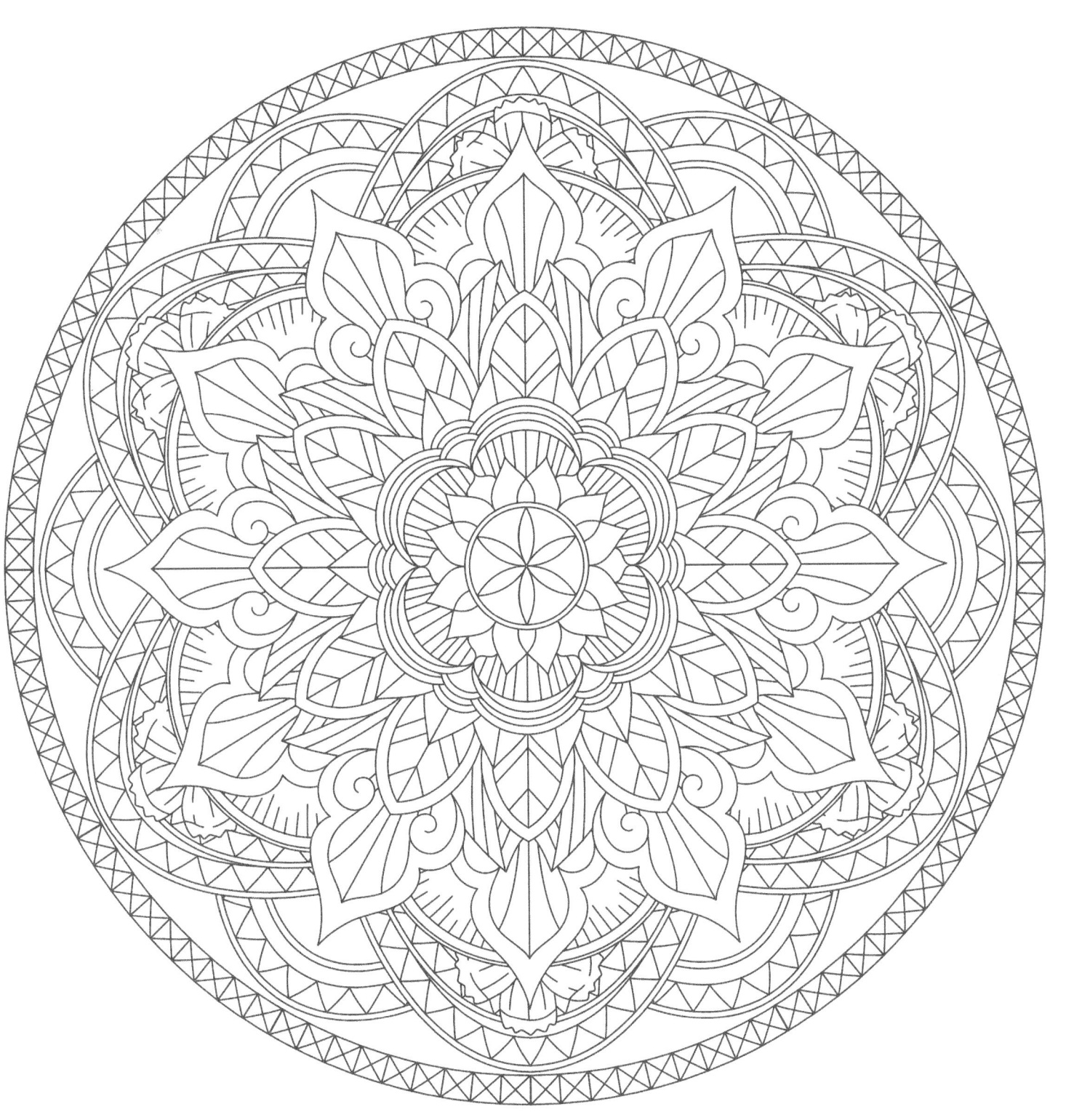

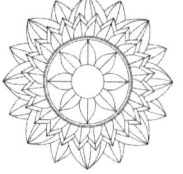

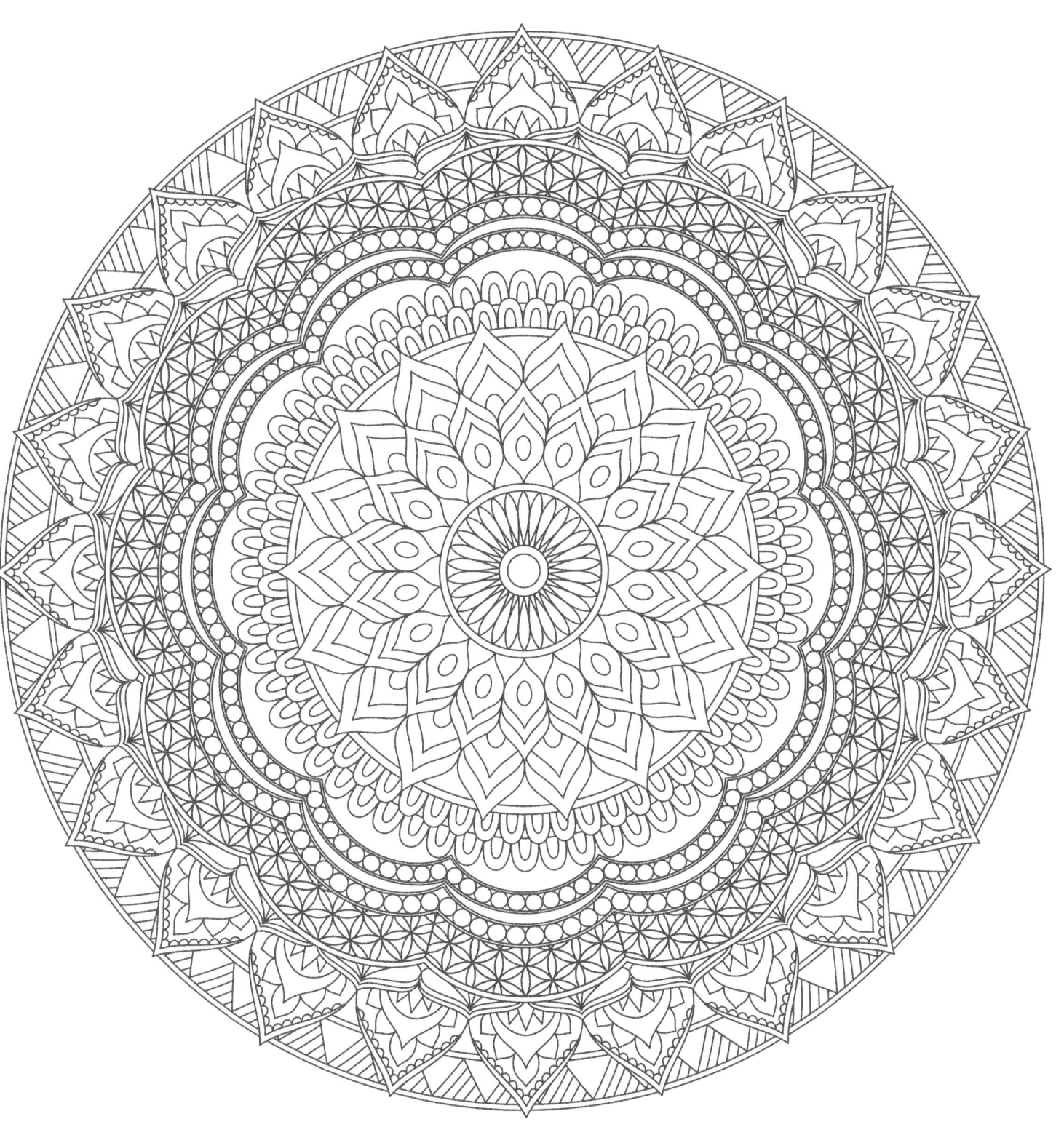

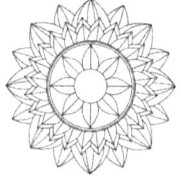

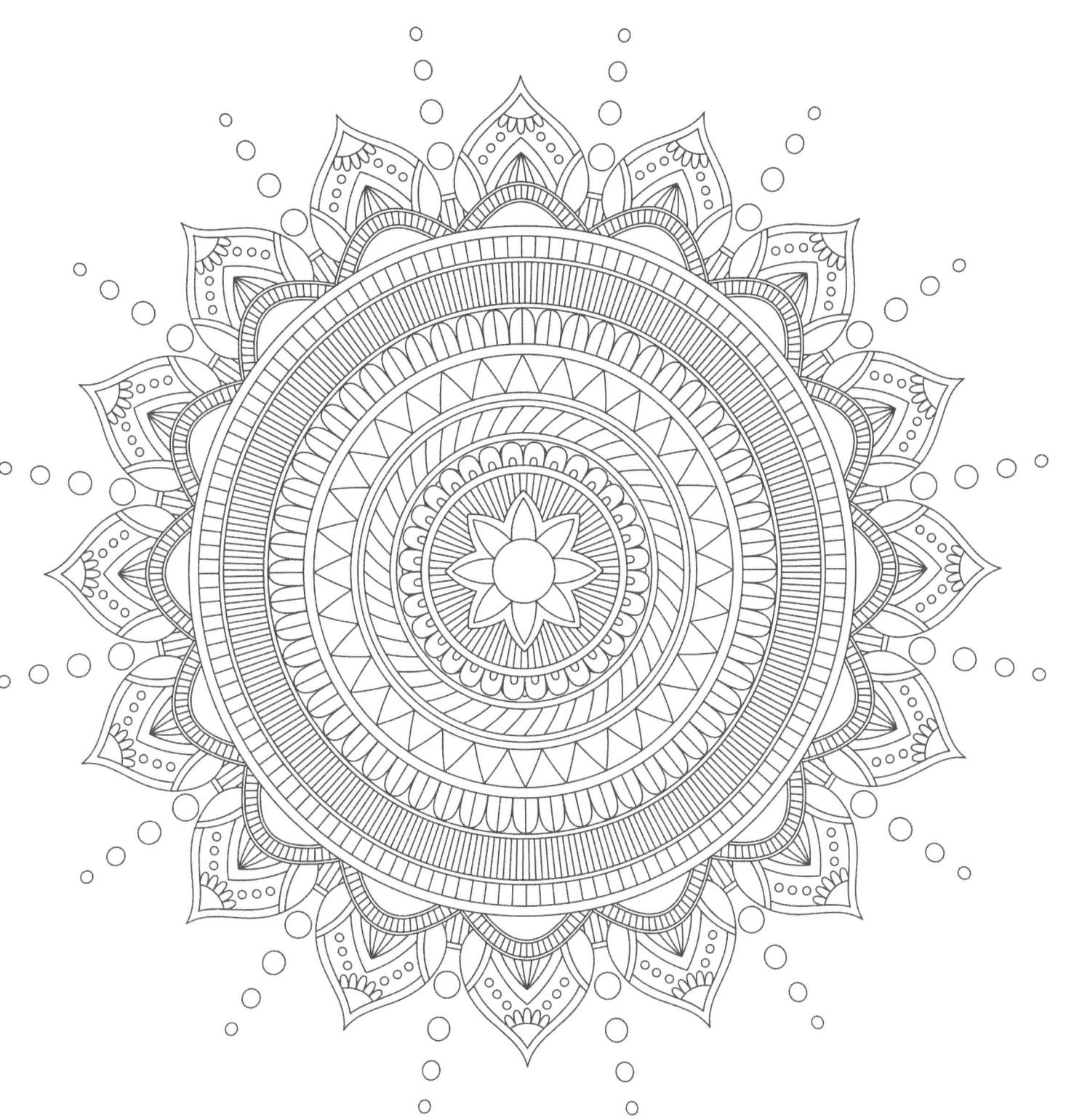

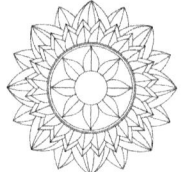

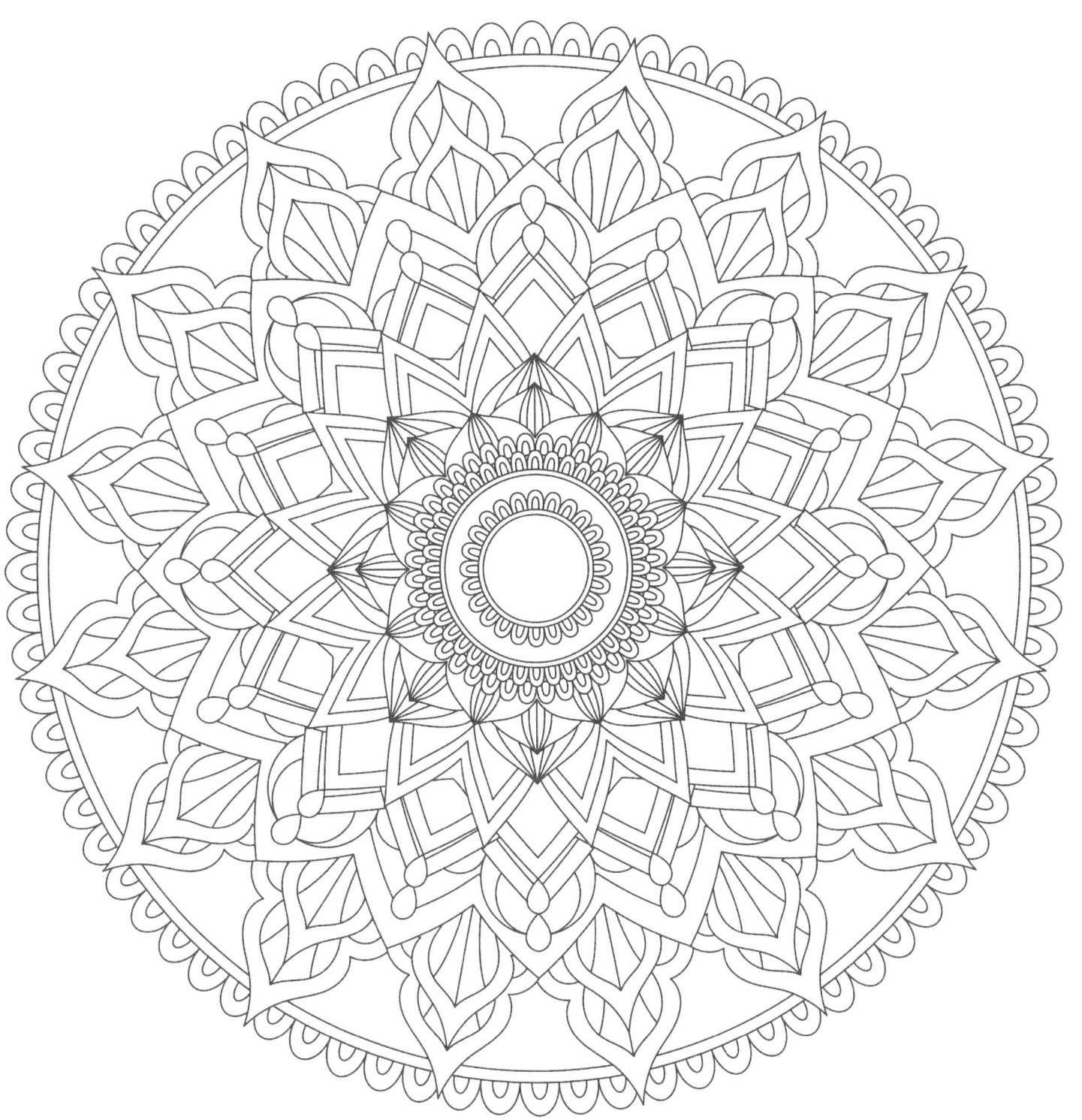

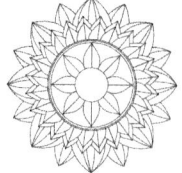

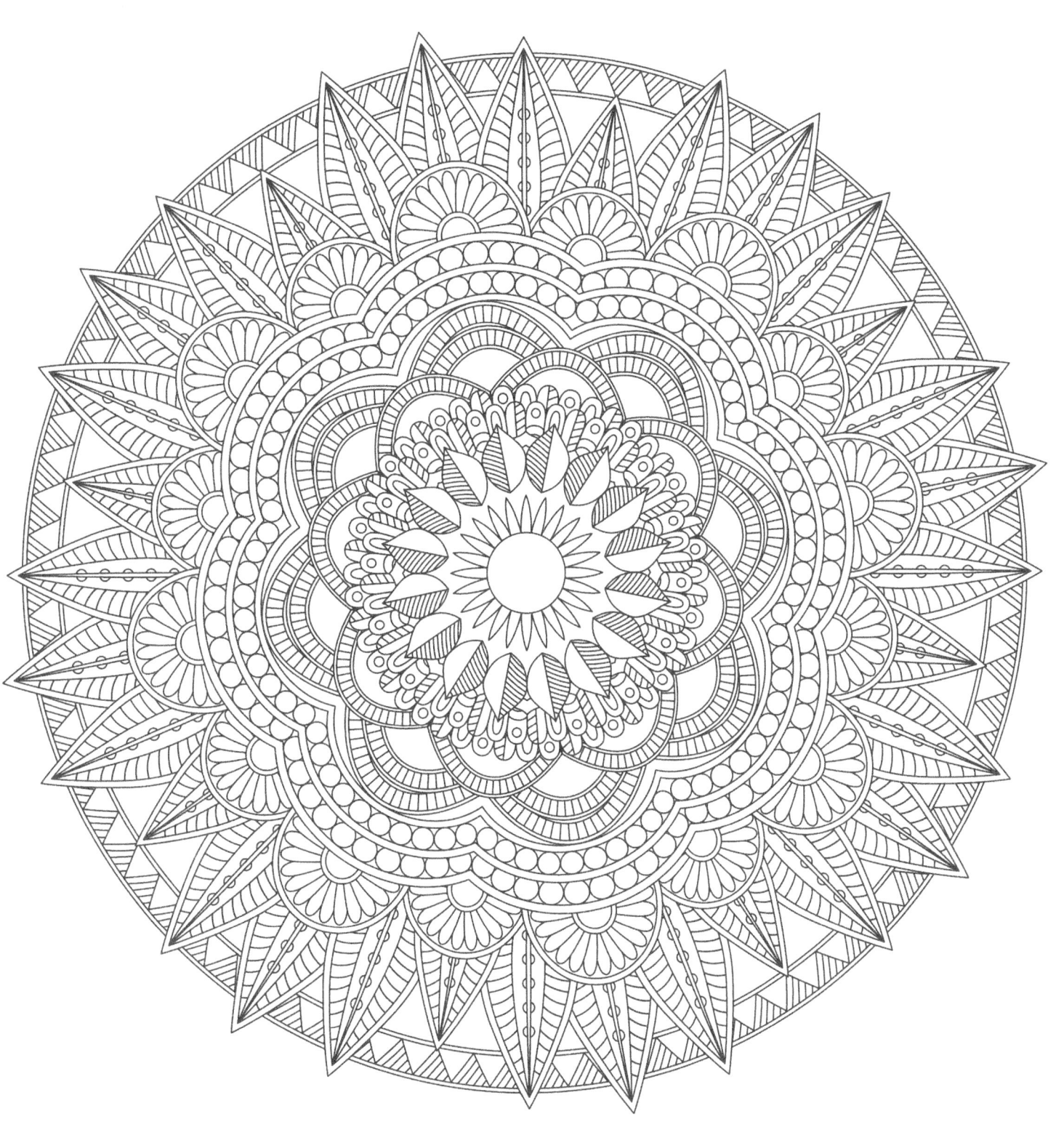

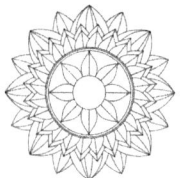

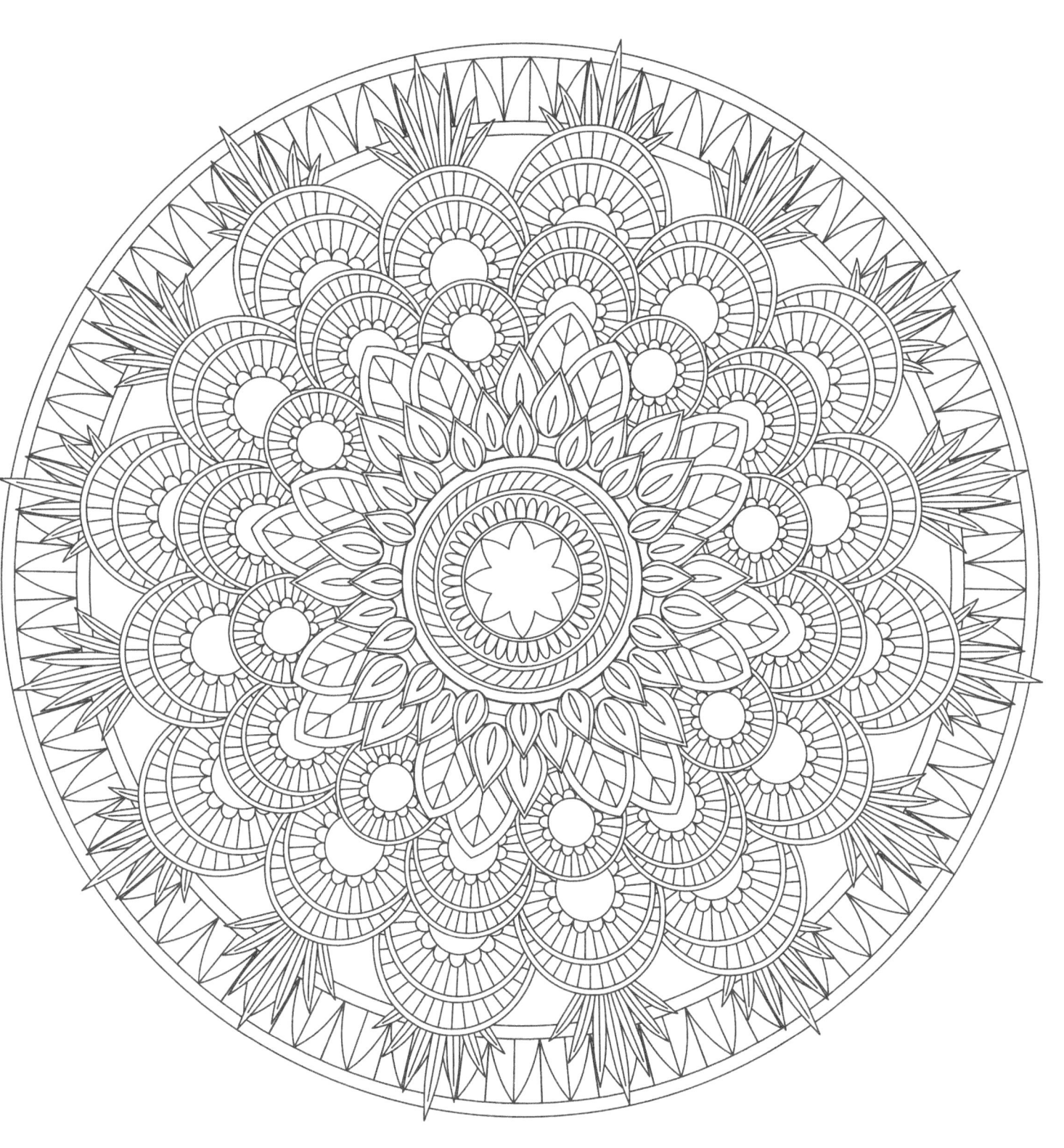

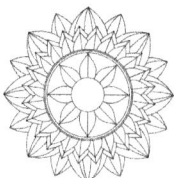

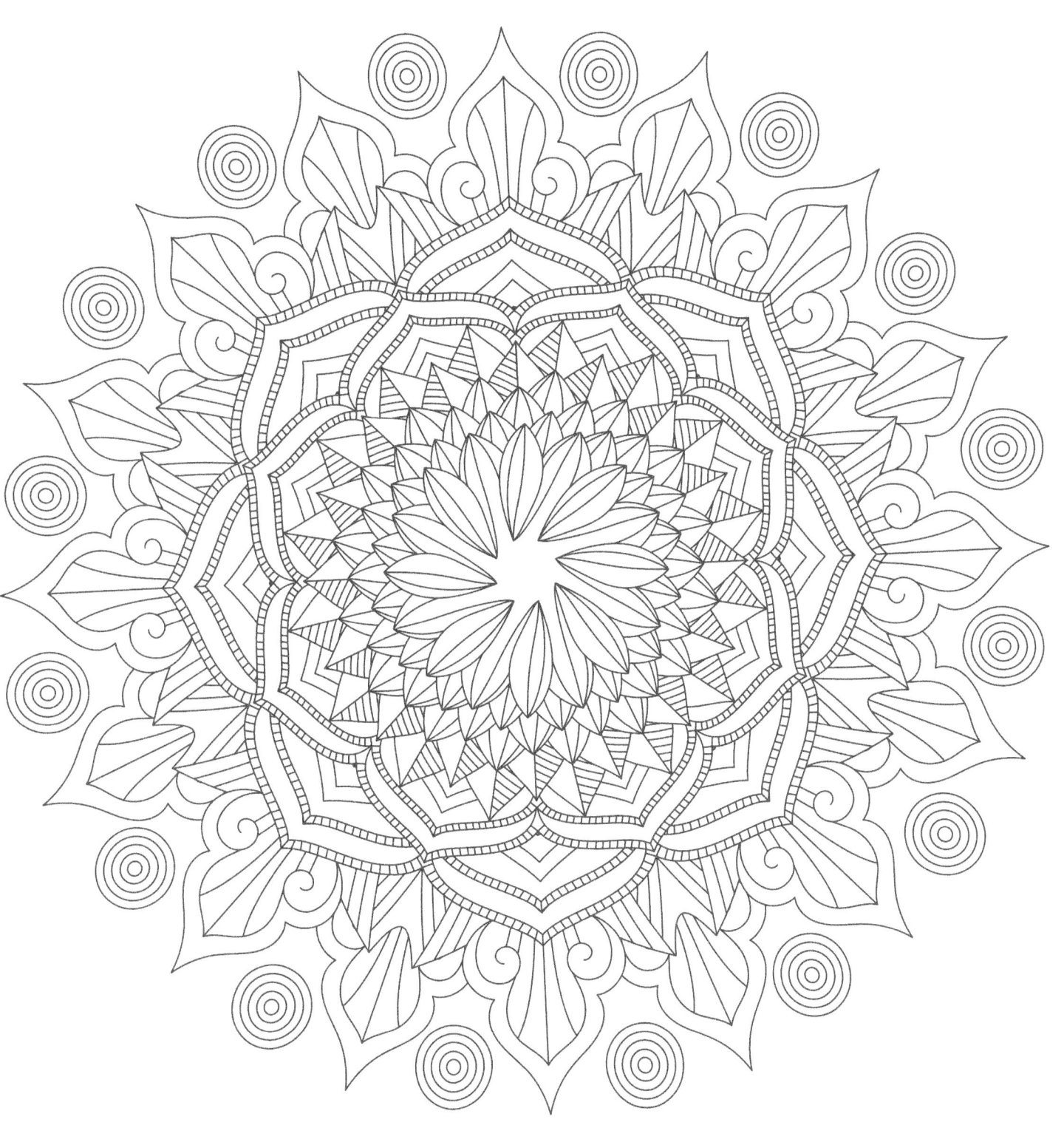

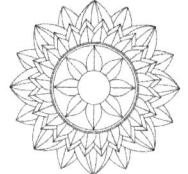

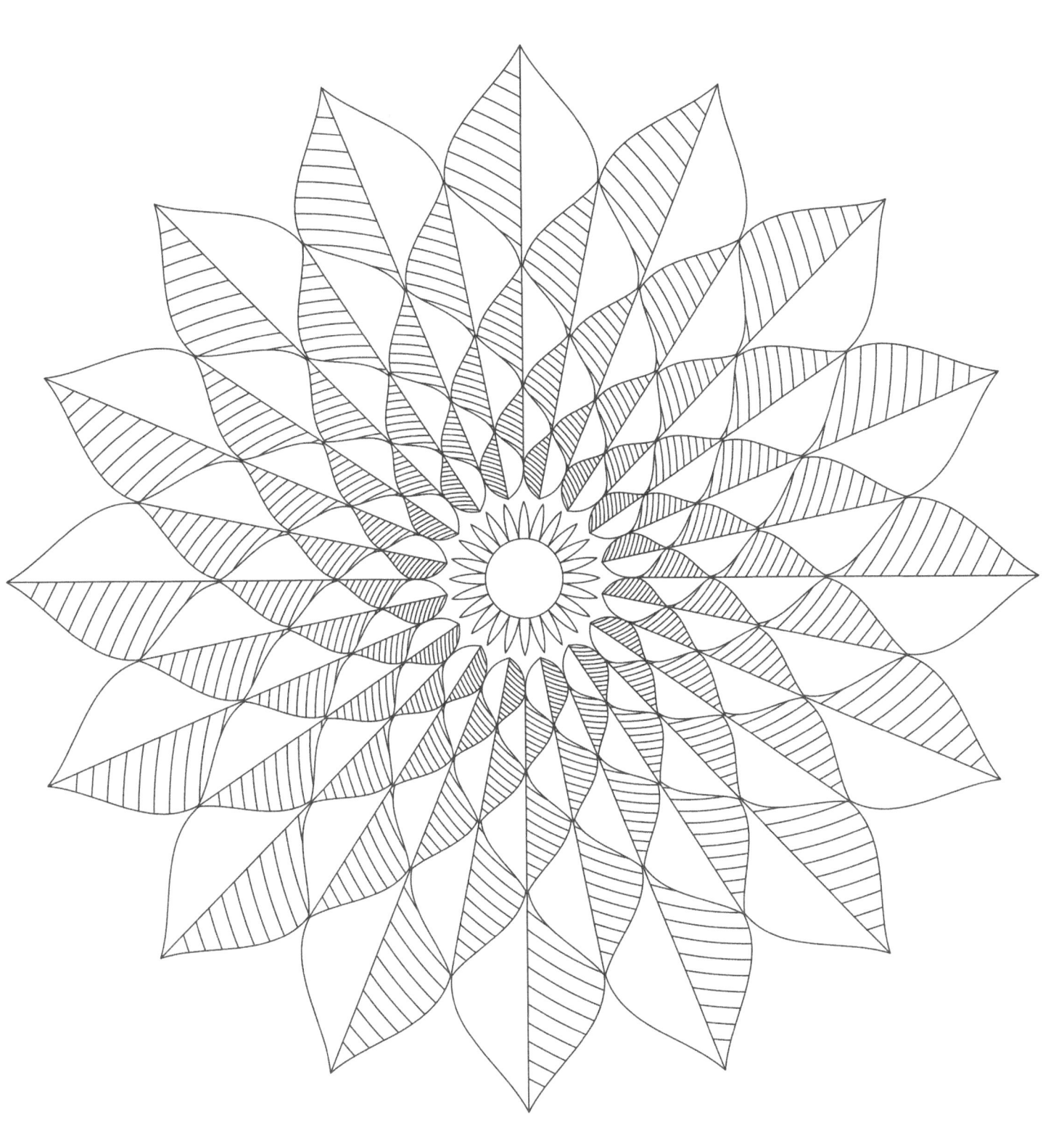

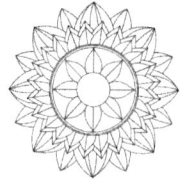

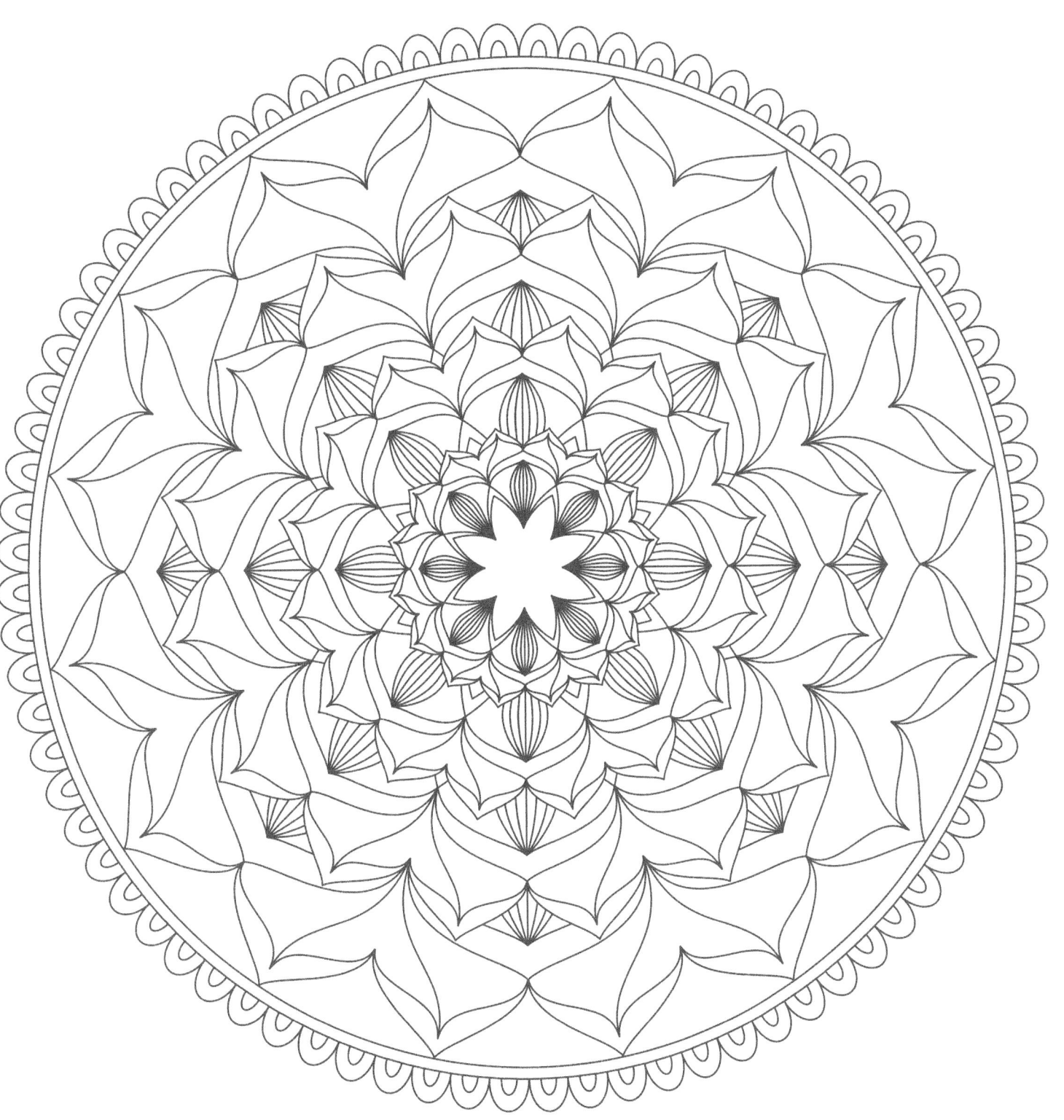

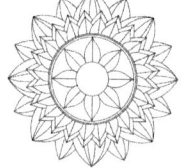

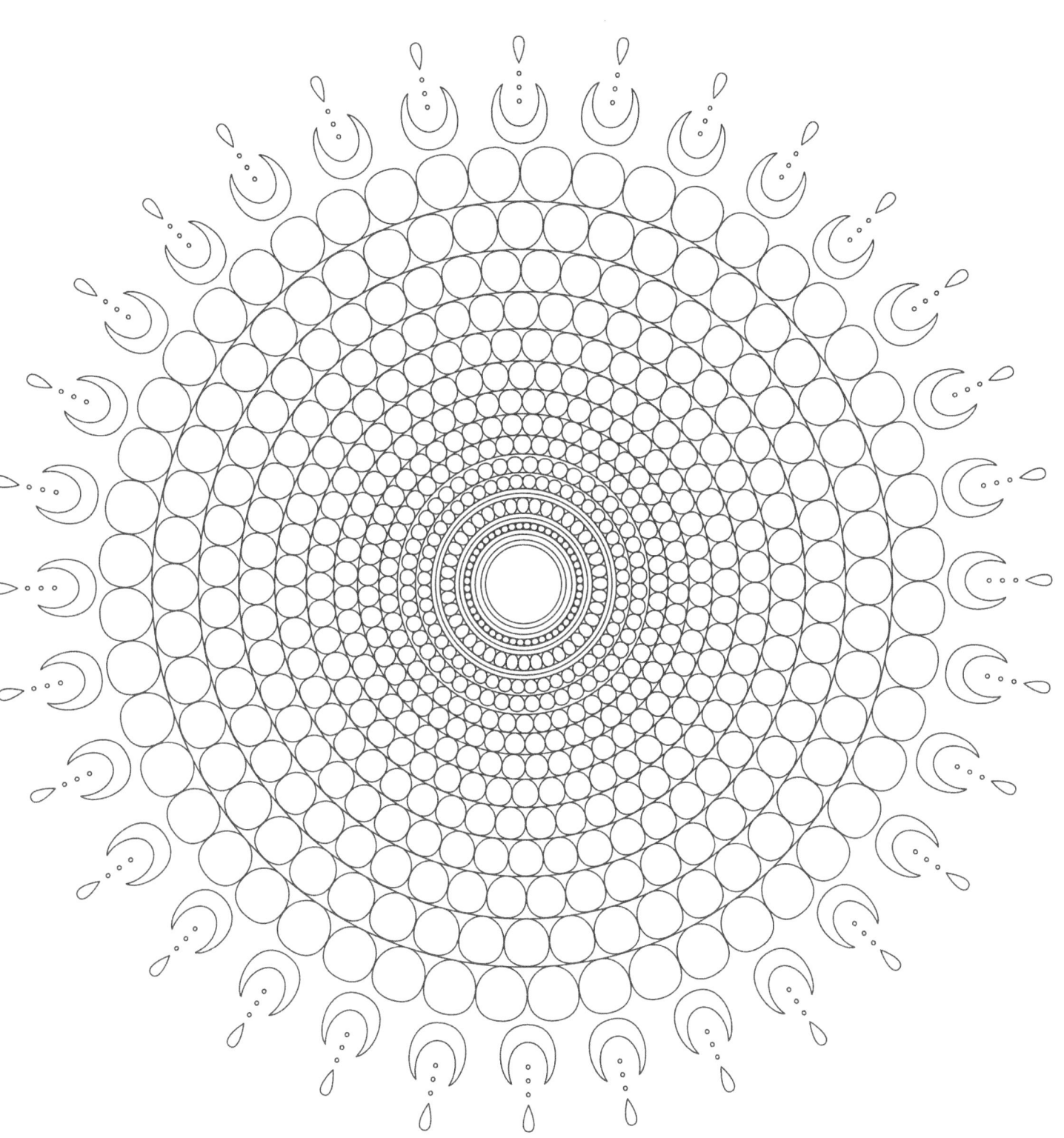

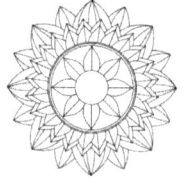

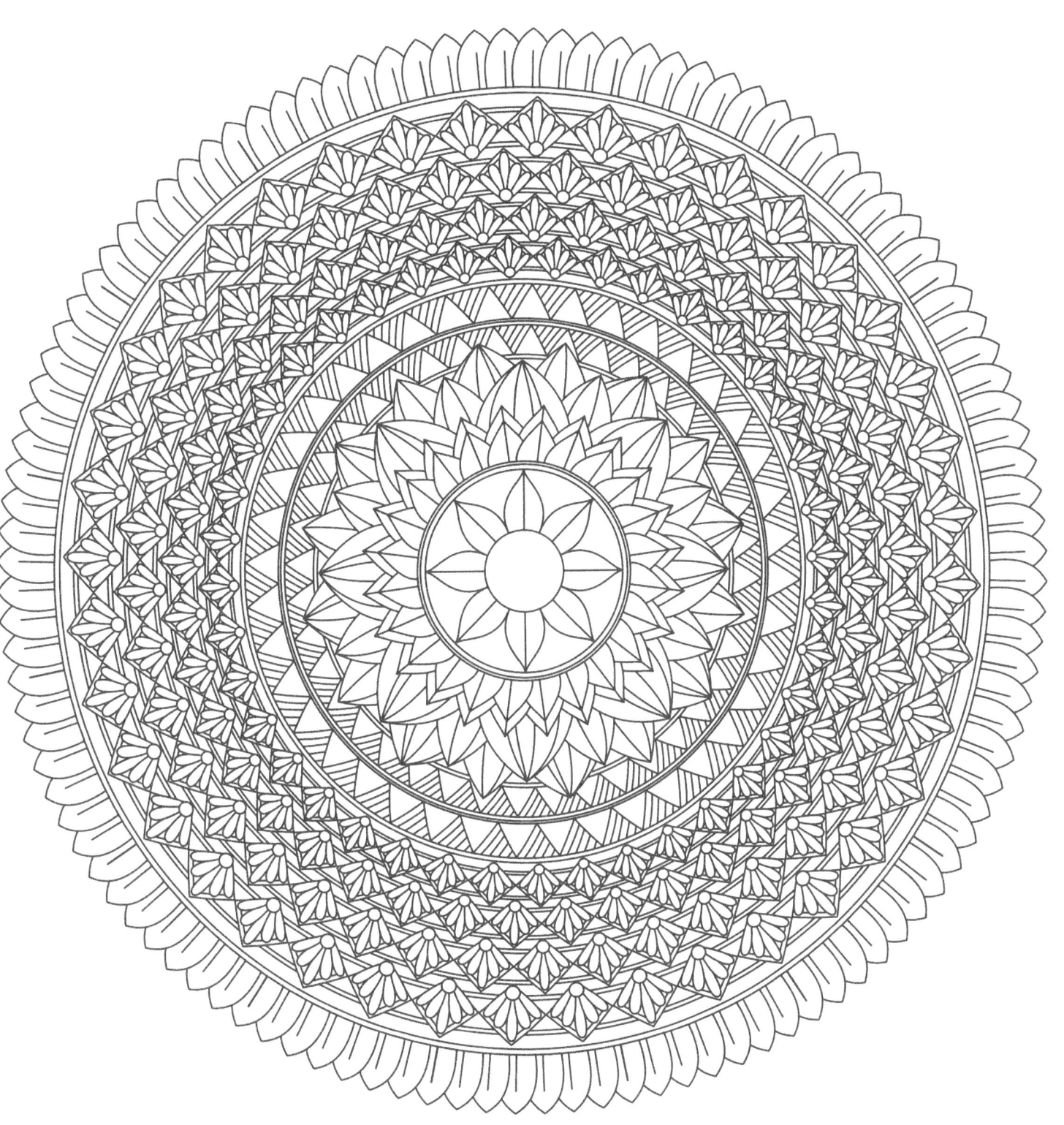

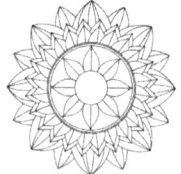

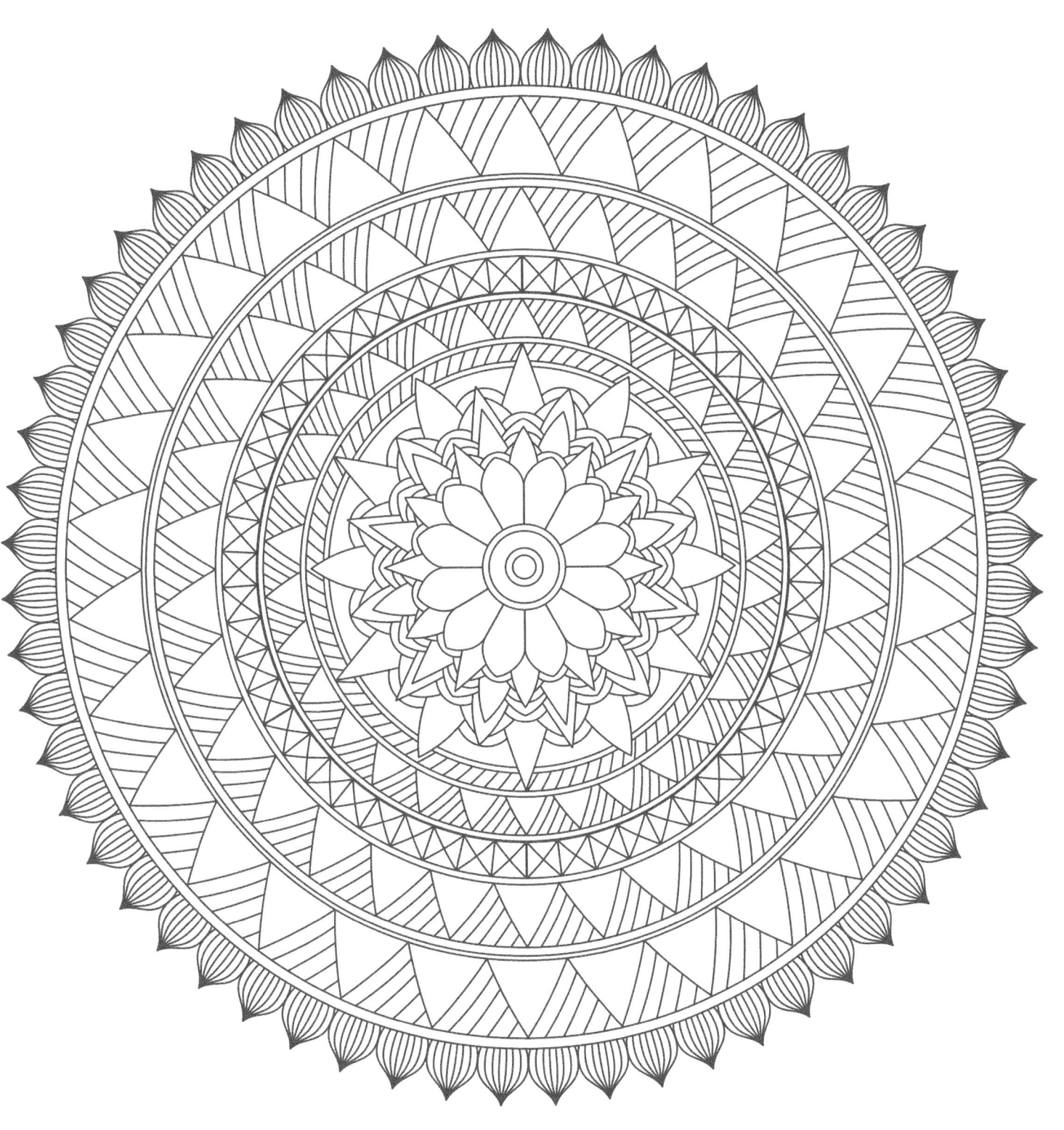

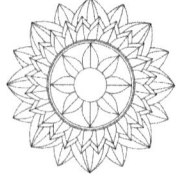

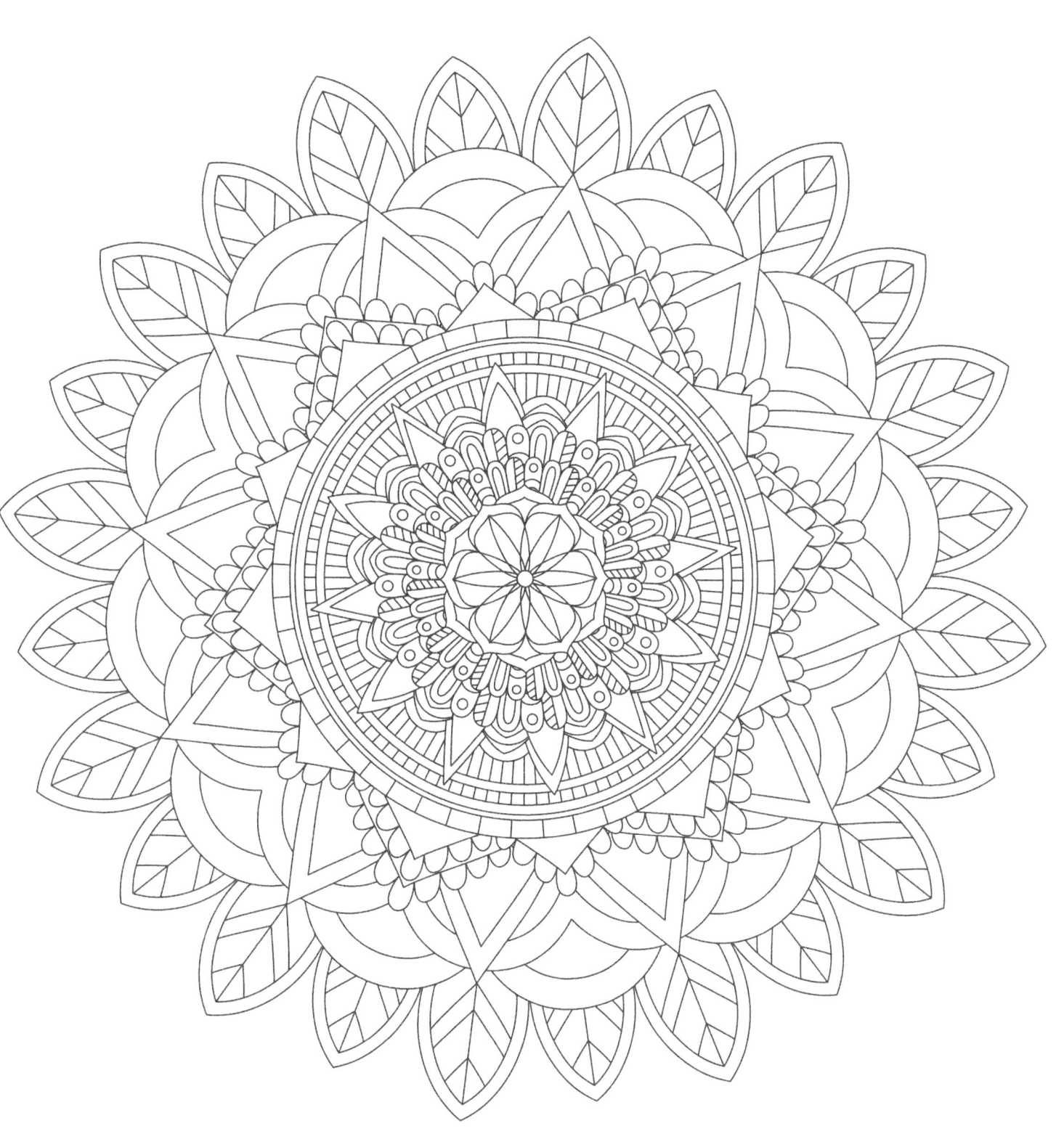

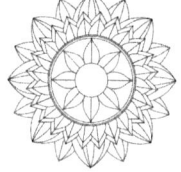

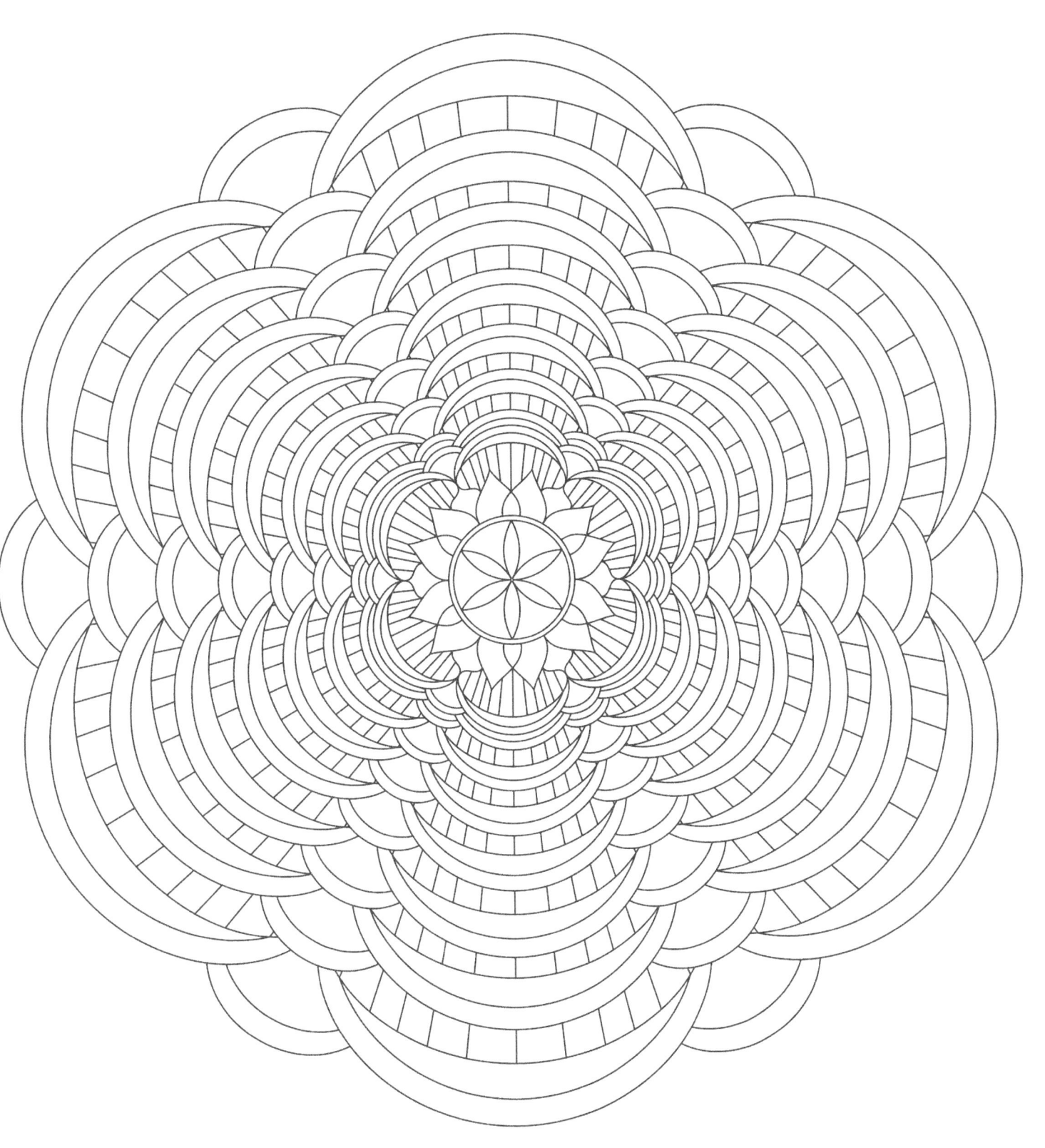

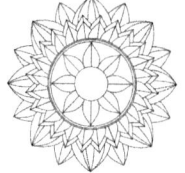

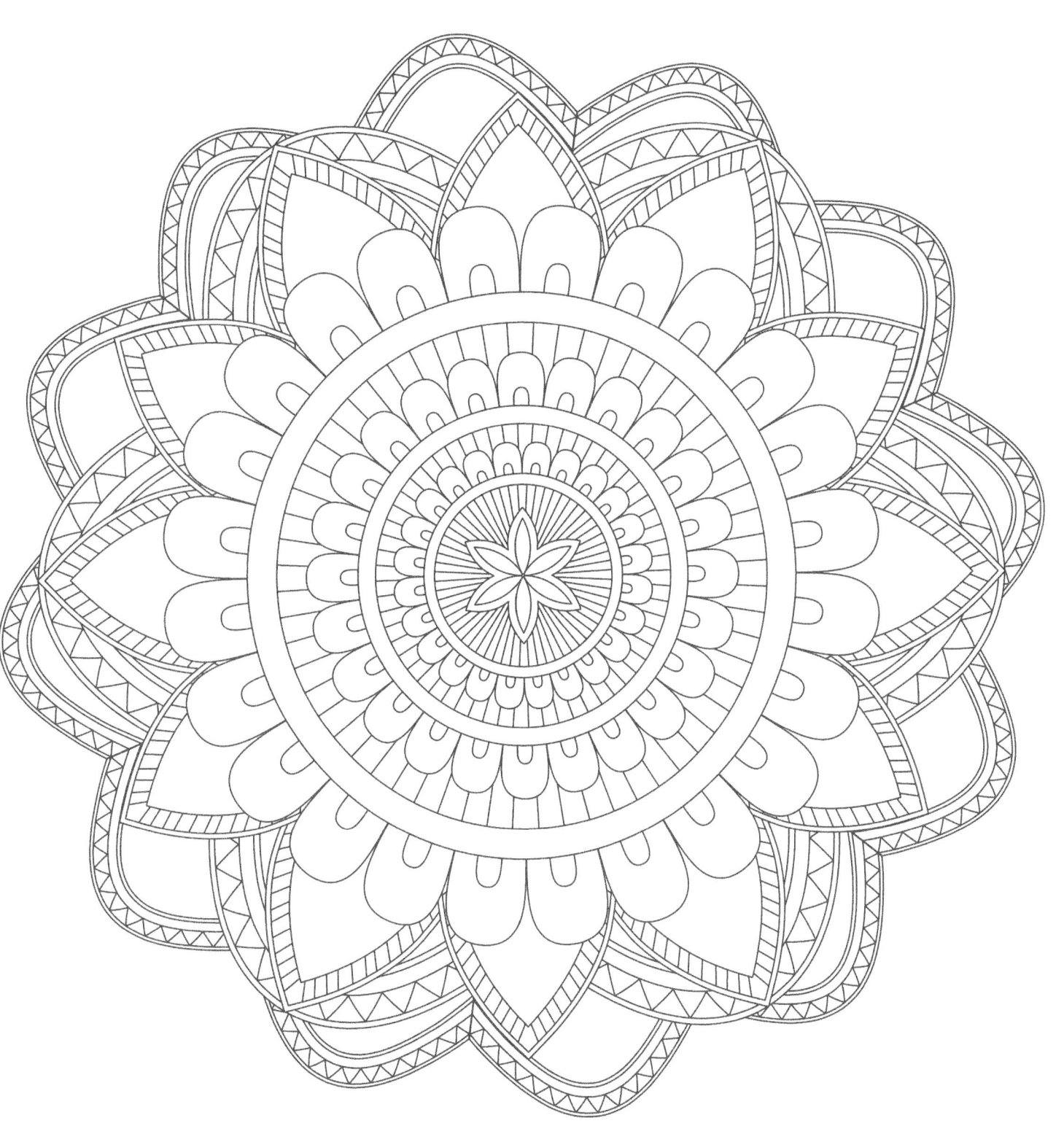

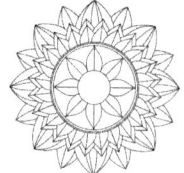

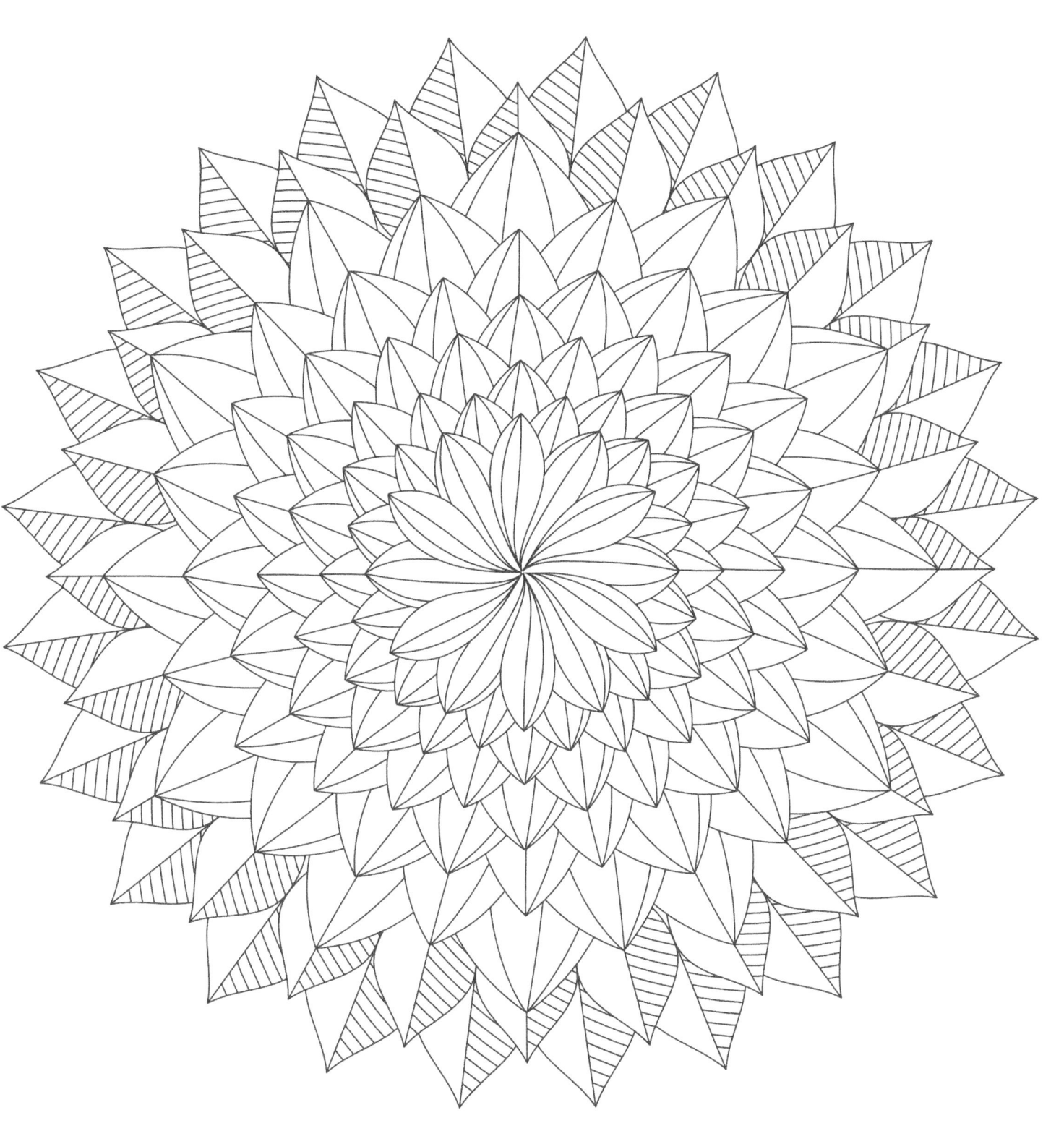

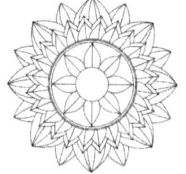

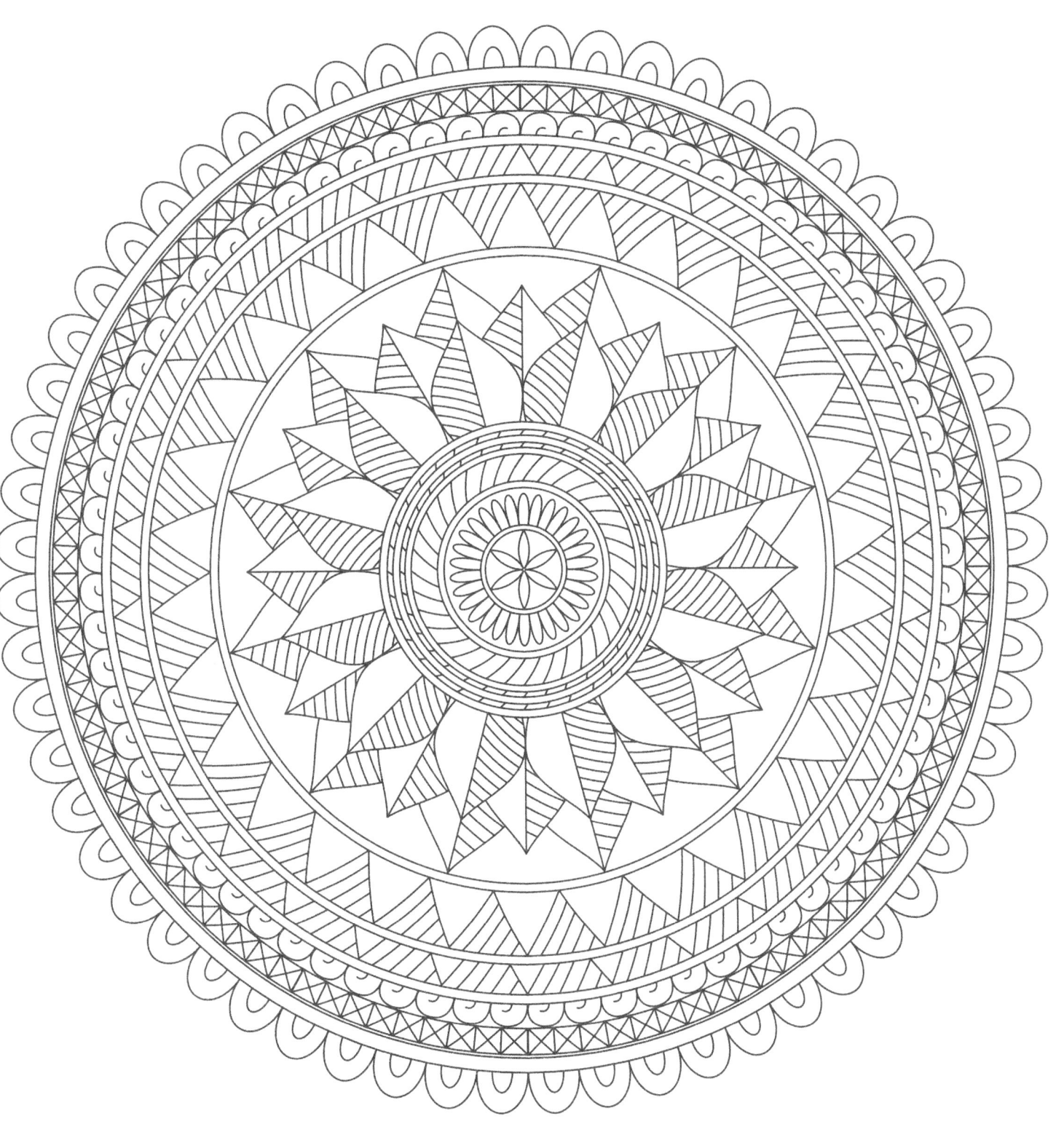

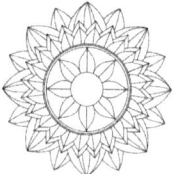

www.ingramcontent.com/pod-product-compliance
Lightning Source LLC
Chambersburg PA
CBHW081102240526
45465CB00026B/3276